# How To Become A Male Stripper

By

Megan Hussey

Edited by Angelicka Wallows

# DISCLAIMER

This publication is meant to offer informative material only. It is sold with the understanding that its contributors are not offering professional service or advice. For any health conditions or questions, you should consult a health professional to diagnose and treat that condition and answer your questions. Before copying any activity described herein, the reader should consult a competent professional for advice.

While the publisher an author have done their best in preparing this book, they make no representation or warranty regarding its contents, and specifically disclaim any implied warranties for any particular purpose. The publisher also assume no responsibility for errors or omissions, and assume no liability for damages resulting from use of information or ideas herein or from following acts described herein. The fact that a person, organization, article or website may be referred to herein as a citation or a possible source of information does not mean that the publisher endorses such sources or their information or recommendations.

Readers should consult an appropriate professional for all physical, mental or health conditions, treatments or questions related to this topic.

~~*~~

# CONTENTS

# PREFACE

Imagine pouting, posing and preening on a luminous stage for a crowd of screaming women, adoring lasses who want you to act the role of their ultimate sexual fantasy. And, furthermore, they're willing to pay for the privilege…

Many men harbor a secret fantasy of working the stage as a male exotic dancer. Yet very few males are actually able to fulfill this decadent dream. Even fewer make a career of erotic dancing, performing at upscale hotels and night clubs around the world, perhaps even on television or in major motion pictures.

So what does it take to succeed in the male exotic dance industry? Well of course you have to be exceptionally attractive in appearance and wickedly seductive in matter. Yet in reality the recipe for beefcake is far more complex. Indeed, how you dress is just as important as how you undress. What you say to a woman is just as important as what you show her. You have to be able to dance, and to talk and tease with proficiency. Most importantly, you must be able to tap in to a woman's deepest, most forbidden, most sensual erotic fantasies, and make them all come true.

Here is a gentle and humorous guide through the world of male exotic dancing. Get the tools you need to succeed in the biz; these tips will earn you some tips, and perhaps a whole new career in the business of pleasing and satisfying women…

# WHY ON EARTH WOULD YOU WANT TO BE A MALE EXOTIC DANCER?

Women. Money. These are just a few of the incentives that lure handsome young men into the sexy and exciting world of male exotic dancing. Ah, but there are so many more perks to this glamorous and lucrative position.

Like more women. And more money.

Seriously though, many gentlemen find that this glamorous career is more like a paid vacation; a paid excuse to party, travel and meet interesting new sexy people. They also enjoy the benefits of a flexible work schedule, and possible inroads to a longstanding career in the arts and entertainment field.

Everyone has to start somewhere, and a number of well-known male celebrities started right here, like for example:

Hollywood superstar Channing Tatum

Born April 26, 1980, Channing is an American actor and film producer, best known for his roles in Step Up (2006), G.I. Joe: The Rise of Cobra (2009), Dear John (2010), The Vow (2012), 21 Jump Street (2012), and Magic Mike (2012). He has also appeared in films such as Coach Carter (2005), She's the Man (2006), A Guide to Recognizing Your Saints (2006), Fighting (2009), and The Dilemma (2010). While known for his dramatic performances in Dear John and The Vow, he has also ventured into more comedic roles. Standing 6'1" (1.85 m), earlier in his career he worked variously as a dancer, model, and stripper.

### TV presenter and actor Mark Consuelos

Mark was born in Zaragoza, Spain, and grew up in Lebanon, Illinois and Tampa, Florida. He attended Bloomingdale High School in Valrico, Florida and Notre Dame University. While living in Illinois, Mark appeared in "Hello, Dolly" at the Looking Glass Playhouse. Before joining "All My Children" (1970) in February 1995, Mark has guested on television shows such as "Fortune Hunter" (1994) and "SeaQuest 2032" (1993). Mark enjoys traveling to Italy, which he does once a year. His hobbies include working out and playing many sports, particularly softball and soccer. He has one brother, who is a doctor, and a sister, who is a lawyer.

### Marcus London

Marcus London made his debut in the porn industry in 2005. It is likely that this performer, who is well-liked among both male and female audiences, got his stage name from his hometown of London, England. Not only is he a photogenic performer with a well-crafted physique, he is also a producer and writer. In January 2007, he married fellow porn star Devon Lee in Las Vegas, Nevada, after dating for eight months. During the course of his career, he received two AVN awards for his work in 2007 and 2010.

### Evan Stone

Born Thomas Ryan in July 18, 1964, Evan is an American pornographic actor. In 2002 he married Jessica Drake, whom he has since divorced. Stone's occasional work outside the pornography industry includes his role as "Jimmy" in the 2007 original series The Lair. In February 2005, Stone hosted cable television program Spice Hotel on Friday, Saturday and Sunday evenings on Spice Live, which focused on porn star couples. In 2011, he was named by CNBC as one of the 12 most popular stars in porn, being the only man on the list. Stone, along with Lee Stone, performed graphic sex scenes with former TNA and WWE wrestling superstar Chyna, in the vivid release Backdoor to Chyna, in 2011. Stone currently resides in Los Angeles, California.

### Mark Davis

He was born on 6 August 1965, in Essex, England, United Kingdom and is a British-born Canadian pornographic actor, a pornographic film director, and an exotic dancer. Mark and his family moved to Toronto, Canada, in 1981. After graduating from high school, he then moved to Los Angeles, California, to shoot a Playgirl pictorial. From 1984 to 1988, Davis was employed as a stripper for the "Chippendale" dancers. In January 1993, Mark began his career in adult films. In 2004 Davis was inducted into the XRCO Hall of Fame and is also a member of the AVN Hall of Fame.

So it obviously pays to be a male exotic dancer, in more ways than one. Yet how does the enterprising gentleman go about entering this exciting field? Read on for more details.

# TIP #1
# THE RECIPE FOR BEEFCAKE

In order to succeed as a male exotic dancer, a man has to be really, really good looking.

"Um, OK," you're probably thinking at this point, "that's like saying that one has to be really, really smart to be an astrophysicist. I laid down good money for this book to pick up these pearls of ever so priceless wisdom."

OK, point taken. The fact remains, however, that only exceptionally attractive men should consider a longstanding career in the male exotic dance field. A male stripper stands as the living embodiment of a woman's ultimate fantasy. She wants to be able to touch, flirt, and dance with a man who looks as though he just stepped out of her wildest fantasy or most decadent dream; perhaps off of the silver screen, or from the steamy pages of an erotic romance novel.

Therefore, it stands to reason that a man with a handsome face and a chiseled, muscular body stands a good chance of attaining success as a male exotic dancer.

### Perfect face

A gorgeous face is something that one is generally born with, though these days even the manliest of men can enhance his features with the help of face creams (FaceLube Ultra Masculine Men's Anti-Aging Face Care Kit or eb5 Face Formula for Men), moisturizers (Neutrogena Men Age Fighter Face Moisturizer or CLINIQUE by Clinique Skin Supplies For Men:Maximum Hydrator), and even cosmetics made for males (The Men Pen, Matte For Men Man Powder or 4voo Shimmer Tint Bronze). Leading cosmetics companies such as Clinique and 4VOO offer special product lines for men only; check 'em out!

### Perfect body

Male strippers often spend their nights at the club and their days at the gym; a daily workout regime is pretty much needed to build those muscles women love. Yet what exactly you do at the gym depends on your personal schedule regarding exercise and body maintenance. Instead of just walking in the door and grabbing the biggest weights available, arrange a consultation with a trainer employed at this facility. He/she — after a quick question and answer session – will tell you what type of, and how many exercises you have to do to get in top shape, reaching the optimum weight and physical condition for your body type. Finally, they may be able to point you in the direction of exercise and dance classes that will help you both build your body and sharpen your skills.

The use of weights is a virtual certainty, but many dancers also do limb stretching exercises and yoga. Flexibility is important for any category of dancer. And some men like aerobic dancing; it may seem redundant to dance in preparation for a dance career but hey, whatever works!

Let me share with you here the Chris Hemsworth official workout plan for Thor. Well, when you want to look like a god, better follow what deities do!

<u>Thor Workout Part 1 : 8 week bulking plan</u>
*How to do it:*
Week one – sets 4 reps 4-6

Week two – sets 4 reps 6-8

Week three – sets 4 reps 8-12

Week four – sets 4 reps 4-6

Repeat for weeks five to eight

*Session one – chest and back:*

Bench press

Bent-over row

Weighted pull-up

Weighted dip

*Session two – legs:*

Squat

Deadlift

Hamstring curl

*Session three – arms:*

Weighted chin-up

Close-grip bench press

Thor Workout Part 2: 4 week fat loss plan

*Circuit one – Tabata (20sec on/10sec off):*

Double kettlebell squats – four rounds

Eight rounds of snatches – eight rounds

*Circuit two:*

Kettlebell swings – 30sec two-hand, 30sec right-hand-only swings, 30sec left-hand-only swings, 30sec alternate swings

Cleans – 5 right, 5 left, 4 right, 4 left, 3 right, 3 left, 2 right, 2 left, 1 right, 1 left, then back up to 5 each side for a total of 60 reps with no rest

*Circuit three:*

Turkish get-ups – 5min continuous

Windmill – 5 each side

Along with his difficult workout plan was a strict bodybuilding diet made of clean protein, protein shakes, chicken breasts, carbs, fruit, vegetables and 4-5 liters of water per day.

For protein shake, you may want to consider BSN Syntha-6 Supplements (chocolate and other flavors) along with body building supplements such as Titanium Muscle Gain.

**Perfect attitude**

Also important is a winning and positive attitude. You must at all times show kindness and respect toward the women who form your audience. The woman is your goddess, not just your meal ticket. Flash her a nice smile (try Idol White teeth whitening pen for a Hollywood smile), tell her she looks nice, ask her if she's having a good time and if there's anything you can do to enhance her evening; use "date etiquette" at all times with your patrons.

### The winning attitude mindset:

*Passion — Desire is the fuel to reach your true potential. Look for the driving force deep inside you.*

*Belief — Believe in yourself and in your success.*

*Strategy — Plan your life as a game, design your path to success as a straight line.*

*Clarity of Values — Values let you believe in something with passion; find your own and stick to them.*

*Energy — Physical, spiritual and mental power do make you successful.*

*Bonding power — Understand that we all see the world differently and keep this in mind when communicating with others.*

*Mastery of communication – Take charge and run your own mind.*

A winning and positive attitudes determine how well you do and how far you go in life.

Your mind is like a garden; whatever you plant, it will get back to you. Plant negative thoughts and nourish them, and your life will be filled with negative things. On the contrary, think positive and your life will be positive.

You always must do your best to tease, spoil and pamper her like a real gentleman. Open doors and pull out chairs whenever possible, and — whenever time allows — stop, to give each audience member special treatment. Even if she doesn't want a lap dance, try to dance close in front of her, making intimate eye contact, showing her the goods up close, hugging her and rubbing her shoulders. If you can pull her from her seat to treat her to a close romantic dance or whirl around the floor, she'll be especially thrilled.

And if you can manage to make her laugh — for the right reasons at least — then all the better! Women love a sense of humor, so the advantage will lie with a dancer who can tell a good joke or pull a funny face.

This may sound like a tall order, but if you have both the look and the persona to make it as a male stripper, then you'll find that all the work was worth it.

~~*~~

# TIP #2
## YOU'VE GOT THE LOOK (!)

OK, so you are really good looking and still want to be a stripper. But what precisely does a male stripper look like? The answer to this question varies greatly from dancer to dancer.

**Diversity**

When a woman attends a male exotic dance show, she is likely to see a group that is rich and diverse in appearance. The first dancer might be a bodybuilder with short spiked hair and golden skin; the gentleman who follows him might be a blossoming business executive with a lean muscled build and a feathered do. The third dancer might be a collegiate athlete with nature made muscles and a boyish grin. And the stunning stud who dances the finale might be a sexy long-haired rocker with tattoos, earrings and leather jeans.

When one thinks about it, these gents don't have much in common aside, of course, from their gorgeous looks and their ability to make women's hearts race.

You do not have to look like a pro wrestler, or for that matter like a plastic male fashion doll, to be a successful dancer. Every female has a different type; therefore, every attractive and eye catching man is sure to appeal to a segment of his intended audience.

And to put it simply; every hot guy has a shot at making it as a male exotic dancer... well, almost. The sad fact of the matter is that not every dude can doff his duds for dollars — OK, could we fit any more d words into the context of one sentence... well, perhaps one more! ;-) — A guy who is substantially over or underweight may want to consider another profession, though if he has an attractive face and a winning persona, he may be able to work out to work his way up, and into the upper echelons of the male exotic dance industry.

### Grooming

Similarly, a well-built man who lacks stunning features may still find a way to make it; the right hair style, a pair of contact lenses, a good acne cream (such as Revitol Acnezine), may be just the right key to his success.

You may elect to wear man make up, now available through a number of cosmetics companies. For while you are not likely to see a male exotic dancer sporting red lipstick or heavy mascara, they will wear eye liner to bring out their peepers (Jean-Paul Gaultier Sharp Eyes Brown Kohl Pen), neutrally colored lip gloss to moisturize and glamorize their mouth (Nivea for Men Replenishing Lip Balm), and powder or foundation to cover any flaws and bring a certain glow to their skin.

Tone, tweeze (Braun Cruzer 5 Body Shaver), cream (Hair Removal by Dermology) or wax (Gigi Brazilian Waxing Kit) so you can tempt and tease the ladies, in order to maintain the level of beauty needed to flourish as a peeler.

Visit a local cosmetics counter, beauty salon, or image consultant for a man makeover. Also consult fashion magazines such as Esquire and Men's Vogue for tips on how to dress and groom for optimum effect.

Do not be surprised if your daily beauty routine becomes strikingly similar to that of the lady in your life. After a good night's sleep, you might rise to wash and moisturize your face, remove unwanted hair, wash and condition your hair, put some lip moisturizer on, apply a day cream on your face, and lay out your clothes for the day. Then after a healthy breakfast, vitamins and protein shake, it's off to the gym or to the local park for a session of jogging or biking. Thus sets the course for a healthier and sexier life and a great new career.

**Beauty**

While a man does not have to be 18 — or, for that matter, even 25 — to excel in this business, you probably shouldn't be too far past your 35th birthday, unless, of course, your look manages to transcend your age (did you think of George Clooney as well?).

There are, naturally, exceptions to every rule, and the same holds true of the exotic dance industry. Granny peelers and chubby strippers of both genders have managed to carve out their own special niche in the industry, as have nerd strippers, clown strippers, and… OK, better stop the list here as we're about to give ourselves, and all our readers, some major night terrors. It is true, however, that just about anyone who is just dying to take their clothes off for money can find some form of public venue in which to do so.

As a general rule, however, the most successful male exotic dancers are those who also find gainful employment as models, actors and stage performers. If your beauty is your business, or at least a part of it, then chances are you can move your assets and put them to work!

Of course, not every dancer will make the cover of Men's Vogue, or — for that matter — the cover of a DVD movie like Magic Mike. You just need to be able to turn a good number of female heads in your general direction. And if you turn the head of only your wife or girlfriend, no worries. You always can perform for her in the privacy of your own bedroom. She might even tip you for the pleasure!

### Healthy Lifestyle

Furthermore, even the most attractive man has to take care of himself. You must maintain the look that you have worked so hard to develop. You also have to maintain a healthy diet (low in fats and bad carbs, high in vitamins and proteins; think salads over sundaes, lean meats and veggies over burgers and fries). Stay away from deep fried food, and prefer steamed, grilled or sautéed recipes. For fruits and vegetable, prefer them raw or steamed.

Here is a list of healthy food (and super-foods) you can use in your meals without hesitation:

Lean meat

Fish

Ostrich

Broccoli

Cucumber

Tomatoes

Beetroot

Carrots

Celery

Goji berries

Strawberries

Blackberries

Blueberries

Acai Berries

Blackcurrant

Oranges

Apples

Passion fruit

Pineapple

Banana

Olive oil

Curcumin

Ginger

Mushrooms

Rice

Almonds and nuts

Pop Corn

Black and green tea

Wine

Garlic

Onion

Yoghurt

Don't forget food supplements; they help you maintain your good looks with minimal efforts. Go for daily intake of multivitamins (I recommend Centrum as they are fairly priced and of good quality), vitamin E for the skin (Nature Made is quite good), Vitamin B for your hair (Nature Made Super B-Complex with Vitamin C and Folic Acid). If you can, include Fish Oil Omega 3, Gingko, Royal Jelly and Ginseng in your list of preferred supplements.

A daily exercise schedule is a must; whether you do regular trips to the gym or you invest in a home gym if you can afford it (Powerline BSG10X Home Gym, 160-Pound

Weight Stack). It may prove to be cheaper in the long run to have your own equipment at home, but it demands more self motivation to train in your house than in the gym. You should also include daily jogging or swimming sessions, which are good for your stamina. For faster results, you may want to take some Creatine Muscle Builder.

You have to wash and condition your hair hair, keeping it neat and tidy at all times. Also do protein treatments (Aramis Protein Enriched Hair Thickener) and comb your strands frequently throughout the day, to keep them free of tangles. Women love well groomed hair that smells nice, and a mouth with white teeth and a fresh breath; they are particularly sensitive to those details, which can be a real turn on… or a turn off! Make it part of your daily routine so that it becomes automatic for you; you will definitely see a difference on how women look at you! Shiny hair and white teeth are your external signs of health and beauty.

### Meal Plan

Most of the guys I know don't like to cook. Fortunately, good nutrition can come without hours of kitchen preparation and tediously planned out Tupperware meals. You can use a microwave, fast-food restaurants and meal-replacement products to help formulate a nutritionally sound and healthy bodybuilding diet. Eating clean doesn't automatically mean bland, boring and inconvenient.

Here is a non-cooking meal plan designed for a 200-pound male bodybuilder, and the overall combination uses the same basic formula: 30%-40% of calories from protein, 45%-55% from carbohydrate and 15%-20% from fat. Simple sugars are kept to a minimum with the exception of the all-important post-workout meal.

<u>Morning Meal</u>

Oatmeal mixed with chocolate or vanilla protein powder always makes for a good breakfast. The combination is low-glycemic with a good balance of protein, carbohydrate and fat. Use 1 cup of slow-cooking dry oatmeal mixed with 1 3/4 cups water. Use a large bowl so it won't boil over. Microwave for two minutes and 40 seconds, then mix in one serving of chocolate or vanilla protein powder. Add a packet of NutraSweet or 1 tablespoon of low-sugar jam to add taste.

If you don't like oatmeal or want something even quicker, try a low-sugar, high-fiber cereal, such as one serving of Grape Nuts mixed with one serving of Fiber One. Add a premixed protein shake as your milk substitute and you're ready to go. This tasty combination has virtually the same macronutrient profile as the oatmeal/protein-powder breakfast and has a relatively low glycemic rating because of the protein and fiber content.

The glycemic index refers to the rate at which carbohydrates, or sugars, are digested and absorbed into the blood. The more quickly a food is absorbed, the higher its glycemic rating. On a scale of 1-100, a highly saturated glucose solution is considered the benchmark for a high-glycemic rating with a score of 100. Foods that rank high on this scale rapidly increase blood-sugar levels, resulting in a large output of the body's energy transport hormone called insulin. Conversely, foods with a low glycemic rating provide slower, longer-lasting energy.

*440 Calories; 35g Protein; 59g Carbs; 7g Fat*

### Morning Snack

Get your next meal in about 2 1/2 to 3 hours after breakfast, generally in the form of a meal-replacement shake or bar. If you choose a shake, select one that has a 1:1 protein-to-carbohydrate ratio or is slightly lower in carbs than protein. Or, you may find the new high-protein/ low-carbohydrate bars to be a little more tasty and satisfying. One whole-food meal option could be two servings of nonfat or 1%-fat cottage cheese and an apple. Of course, the apple could be substituted with peaches, plums, tomatoes, or virtually any green or yellow fibrous vegetable.

You want to keep a steady flow of amino acids going to the muscles at this point. While most glycogen replacement is completed in the 2-3 hours after training, protein needs to be steadily funneled in throughout the day.

*Meal-replacement shake: 260 Calories; 37g Protein; 24g Carbs; 2g Fat*

*Bar: 330 Calories; 30g Protein; 15g Carbs; 6g Fat*

*2 servings cottage cheese with fruit or vegetables: 254 Calories; 29g Protein; 29g Carbs; 2.5g Fat*

<u>Midday Meal</u>

About 2 1/2 hours later, it's time for some real food. The content of this meal depends on your personal preference and your location at the time, but a sandwich is a good choice.

Bread is almost always frowned upon when it comes to bodybuilding nutrition. Many bread products are processed carbohydrates with a very high glycemic rating, but there are exceptions. Rye, pumpernickel and pita bread all have moderate- to low glycemic ratings. Factor in the protein source used in your sandwich (tuna, turkey, chicken) that will lower the glycemic rating, and you have a healthy, relatively low-glycemic meal.

Tuna mixed with nonfat or low-fat mayonnaise on a small pita bread is a fantastic meal, whether you're on the go or at the table. Adding salsa and/or hot peppers gives this sandwich a little zing.

If you don't have time to make a sandwich, a fast-food alternative is as simple as picking up a grilled-chicken sandwich or two. A 200-pound male should get a sandwich with the amount of chicken breast of two sandwiches. Of course, order the sandwiches without mayonnaise, cheese or oil-based dressing, but you can add a small amount of barbecue sauce or ketchup for more taste.

*6 oz. tuna on pita bread: 374.5 Calories; 45.5g Protein; 38g Carbs; 4.5g Fat*

## Mid-afternoon Snack

Some 2 1/2-3 hours later is the last meal you'll eat before your training session. Not only does it need to be convenient, but your body should have little difficulty digesting it. If you guessed this would be the ideal time for a meal-replacement shake, you're right. If the thought of a shake doesn't excite you, a nonfat, no-sugar-added yogurt mixed with one serving of protein powder will do just fine.

*Meal-replacement shake: 260 Calories; 37g Protein; 24g Carbs; 2g Fat*
*8 oz. nonfat yogurt mixed with protein powder: 238 Calories; 34g Protein; 21g Carbs; 2g Fat*

## Post-Workout Meal No. 1

Right after you finish your training session, it's time for the two meals that will most influence your bodybuilding progress. The 2-3 hours following your workout are most commonly referred to as the post-workout window of opportunity. This is a period when your muscles are very receptive to storing glycogen (carbohydrates) and absorbing amino acids (proteins). If you use this 2-3-hour period wisely, you'll not only have more energy for your next workout but you'll also fulfill one of the most critical elements involved in adding lean mass; proper post-exercise nutrition.

You should try to consume 80-100 grams of high-glycemic carbs and 25-40 grams of protein in your first meal after your workout. Premade post-workout bars (VPX Zero Impact Protein Meal Replacement Bar) and drinks (American Body Building Speed Stack Nutritional Drink) fulfill these requirements nicely, if not perfectly. This is also the ideal time to take supplements like creatine monohydrate (All Max Creatine Monohydrate) and L-glutamine (NOW Foods L-Glutamine) simply because the absorption rate will be much greater. The correct timing is definitely post-workout.

*1 high-protein/high-carb sports drink and one meal-replacement sports bar: 535 Calories; 26g Protein; 87g Carbs; 5g Fat*

### Post-Workout Meal No. 2*

Your second post-workout meal and final full meal of the day should be consumed 60-90 minutes later. This meal should be rated moderate- to moderately high-glycemic. Remember, you still want to take full advantage of the post-workout window of opportunity. You will want to consume another 80-100 grams of carbs and 30-50 grams of protein in this meal.

At this meal you're allowed to eat various foods that would be off-limits at other times of the day because of the glycemic level of the carbohydrates. Here are several different no-cook combinations that are not only satisfying but really get the job done.

- Healthy Choice French Bread Pizza. Believe it or not, this is a moderately high-glycemic meal that has a perfect post-workout macronutrient profile. You can eat two pizzas. Of course, preparation does require using a microwave oven or conventional stove.

If you want to avoid any preparation, a bagel-based sandwich is an excellent choice. Add 6 ounces of cooked unprocessed deli-style turkey or chicken breast to your favorite bagel. Add mustard, nonfat or low-fat mayonnaise, or any low-fat topping and enjoy. For a few more carbs, you can add two servings of Baked Tostitos or Baked Lays chips to your meal.

- Turkey breast or chicken breast submarine sandwich (Make sure the meat is real, not processed). You will want a large sandwich with extra turkey or chicken.

Use the macronutrient profiles provided and reference a book on food counts and values to come up with plenty of other options. Remember, this is the one meal that allows for a little flexibility.

* Add 1 tablespoon of essential oils each day to satisfy the body's need for essential fatty acids. The oil can be added to a meal or taken in between meals.

*2 Healthy Choice French Bread Pizzas#: 660 Calories; 44g Protein; 98g Carbs; 10g Fat*
*Bagel sandwich and chips: 650 Calories; 46g Protein; 103g Carbs; 6g Fat*

# This product's sodium content may seem a bit high (480-960 mg), but the remainder of the diet presented here is relatively low-sodium. Recommendations for sodium range from 2,000-3,000 mg daily. Athletes, especially hard-training ones, need to make sure they take in enough sodium each day.

Add to it a daily supply of fresh fruits and vegetables. Most recommendations suggest consuming five servings per day; that's a minimum.

Don't forget to add a complete multivitamin/mineral supplements to your daily meal plan. This is just to ensure that you get all the vitamins and minerals you need for recovery, growth, digestion, and overall health and well-being.

Please note that this meal plan is for bodybuilding purposes, and should only be used after consulting with a nutritionist. Once you have achieved the lean body you wanted, you should then adapt your diet again to maintain your results.

# TIP #3
## DANCING WITH THE STUDS

As important as one's appearance is to their overall success as a male exotic dancer, the fact remains that some very successful actors and male models are not able to make the grand transition to the role of professional stripper.

"Why," you may ask, "would a sexy, gorgeous and generally hawt young man be turned away from the stage of a leading male revue?"

Well, to put it simply; tough guys don't dance, and neither could they.

Just as not every woman who looks like a song bird was meant to warble a tune, not every gorgeous model can cut a rug or, for that matter, cut it in a G-string.

You do not have to be Mikhail Baryshnikov or Fred Astaire to be a male stripper. Yet you should have a certain sense of rhythm and be able to keep a beat. No need to pirouette, but you must know how to prance; you don't have to excel in ballet, provided that you can move your booty!

### The references

It goes without saying that anyone who has a dance background, or who is employed as a professional dancer, will have an automatic edge in this field. Barring this, however, an aspiring stripper could learn some basic steps in a dance class, or through an online course or DVD-based dance instruction program (such as The Art of Exotic Dancing: Striptease Series - Male Exotic Dancing). A ballroom or ballet dance class might be particularly beneficial, as their brand of artistic movement is known for its high level of intimacy and romance. A disco class will teach you to hoof it with confidence and sexiness, a la John Travolta in Saturday Night Fever. Hip hop moves are slick and trendy, and belly dancing (yep, these days tough guys do belly dance) is perhaps the ultimate form of divine sensual expression.

If the pole dancing and burlesque classes conducted in your area are open to male students, then by all means take them. There you will learn the art of seduction as expressed in the form of dance steps.

Beyond classes and instructional DVDs, you can seek further inspiration from performance videos released by major male exotic dance groups such as:

The Chippendales

La Bare

Manpower Australia

The Men of Playgirl

The Hollywood Men

The Hollywood Bad Boys

The London Knights

The Dreamboys UK

Or watch any of the handful of films that feature male strippers as their (ahem!) titular heroes. These include:

Magic Mike

A Night in Heaven

For Ladies Only

Just Can't Get Enough

Ladykillers

Certain erotic DVDs, such as Malerotic 1 and 2, Love Scenes volume 1 through 4, Bachelorette Party, and a number of Playgirl titles feature longer and more explicit strip scenes, as do straight hardcore XXX films entitled Fuckingdales on Tour and Club Exotica part 1 and 2 (or so we've heard!)

And if you are just too much of a dude to check out any of those woman-directed titles, it might be reassuring to know that a number of mainstream (and very macho) comedies just happen to feature male exotic dance scenes. These include: Summer School, Bachelor Party, Gimme an F, Sensations, Pecker, Mr. Mom, and Deuce Bigalow: Male Gigolo.

Other films — such as Staying Alive, Dirty Dancing, Dance with Me, Salsa, Lambada, and the Step Up series — all feature talented male hoofers who do not have to strip to seduce.

The list is long and if you don't want to purchase all of these movies, you can always watch them online on Netflix. So let me offer you a free month trial via this link:

**http://bit.ly/NETFL30**

## The moves

At the very least, the aspiring stripper should seek to master a few basic steps:

*Body roll:*

The body roll is the most basic of stripping maneuvers; it is relatively easy to learn and do. Basically the gentleman sways his body slowly forward from the shoulders downward, emphasizing the smooth shift of his chest and hip muscles. Thus he commences a smooth, slow and seductive undulation sure to leave audience members breathless. For a description and brief demonstration of the body roll, check out this interview with the cast members of the film Magic Mike: http://youtu.be/dxx2J4DkjZ8

*Groin thrust:*

This is the time-honored maneuver in which the gentleman… well… thrusts his groin. Hard, and to the optimum delight of every woman present. Starting from the rear he thrusts his privates forward, again in a smooth, undulating motion; one that simulates the motions of sex. For the best example of a groin thrust, check out the first dance scene in the movie A Night in Heaven in which Christopher Atkins thrusts his way into Lesley Ann Warren's heart — and bed!

*Lap dance:*

And then, of course, there's the lap dance. This signature dance of the erotic industry also qualifies as the one dance that can be performed off of one's feet.

Many people harbor major misconceptions about the nature and character of a lap dance. Some believe, for example, the simple act of shaking and shimmying in front of someone constitutes a lap dance. Others believe that this sensuous maneuver involves actual contact with the genitals of the recipient.

The truth, as with most things, lies somewhere in between. Basically a lap dance is an act akin to dry humping. Lap dance do's include embracing the recipient, staring into her eyes, kissing her cheeks, neck and closed lips, rubbing your hard, sweaty body against hers, and grinding your groin into her lap so she feels the heat. http://youtu.be/3HZcL2bCi3U

Once you have mastered the basics, feel free to practice them at home for your wife or girlfriend. If you're currently single, you might ask a few female friends to be the audience for your first show. By the end of the evening you will have gained some valuable pointers and performance critiques, and maybe even a few dollars in tips!

**The beat**

Of course, as with most forms of movement, the steps are only half the equation when it comes to exotic dance. The music that you choose is also of crucial importance.

"Yeah, right," you might be thinking at this point, "like she's really going to be concentrating on the music when I'm grinding my junk into her face."

OK, point taken — most literally. The fact remains, though, that it would be hard to perform a sexy dance to the tune of a song that is slow, mellow or depressing in theme. One does not want to swivel their hips and wag their tongues (and other body parts) to the soothing sounds of "Love Can Build a Bridge" or "Christmas Shoes".

On the opposite end of the musical spectrum, your female spectators are not likely to appreciate the use of songs that might sound perfectly in place at a female strip show: "Girls Girls Girls", "Crazy Bitch", "Something in Your Mouth," umm, no! And that's putting it nicely. Very much so.

So what songs should provide the scintillating backdrop for a male exotic dance performance?

Read on for some suggestions.

*Classic standards of the 'he-strip':*

"It's Raining Men" by The Weather Girls

"Ladies Night" by Kool and the Gang

"Muscles" by Diana Ross

"You Can Leave Your Hat On" by Joe Cocker

Modern, very sexy dance beats:

"Scream" by Usher

"Sexy and I Know It" by LMFAO

"Your Body" by Christina Aguilera

"Irresistible" by Jessica Simpson

"You Drive Me Crazy" by Britney Spears

"Give It Up to Me" by Sean Paul.

The seductive lyrics and hard-pounding beats of these songs are bound to leave women breathless.

*Metal:*

Anything by Black Veil Brides or Reckless Love — they're solid musicians and, hey, women love them.

"Flesh and Blood (Sacrifice)" by Poison

"Take It Off" by The Donnas

"Lay It Down" by Ratt

"Smooth Up in Ya" by The Bulletboys

"Lay Your Hands on Me" by Bon Jovi

*Techno and hip hop*

"I Invented Sex" by Trey Songz

"Pony" by Ginuwine (which served as the backdrop of Channing Tatum's performance in "Magic Mike")

"International Lover" by Prince

"Sexting" by Blood on the Dancefloor

*Europop*

"All She Wants Is" or "Hungry Like the Wolf" by Duran Duran

"Strip" by Adam Ant (naturally!)

Another good choice would be "Obsession" by Animotion or the same song in its original version by Michael Des Barres and Holly Knight; this was the song that Christopher Atkins danced to in "A Night in Heaven".

In selecting the music that will fuel and showcase your delicious dance of seduction, pick a song with a sexy beat that is easy to dance to. Also something shamelessly drenched in sensuality. The lyrics should be provocative and daring, the tune smooth and sensual. The song, in other words, should be the musical embodiment of the man who dances to its sizzling rhythms.

Really, the key to successful male exotic dancing is to use what you have to maximum effect. Flex those muscles, stretch those limbs, gyrate and undulate. Pout, smile, make love to them with your eyes. Follow your primal sexual instincts and do a dance of sheer seduction; a mating dance that will draw the attention and stir the loins of even the most subdued woman. In short, dance to impress.

# TIP #4
## LITTLE THINGS (AND ONE BIG) THAT MEAN A LOT

So you now have the look and the dance steps to make it as a male stripper. You are almost ready to hit the stage… almost, that is.

Before you present yourself to an audience of women, with the ultimate intent to offer skills and body as their most forbidden erotic fantasy, be sure you know exactly what they want, and just how to give it to them.

### Etiquette

Beyond being physically attractive, a good dancer must above all else be the perfect gentleman. Treat each woman with chivalry and respect, respecting her body boundaries (even during lap dances) and watching for signs that she may be uncomfortable. Women come to male strip shows in search of a tease, not a ravishment. Do not under any circumstances touch her private areas (her breasts, her vagina, her pubic area, her clitoris) or call her a disrespectful name that questions her persona or her sexual morality (bitch, whore, and slut are definitely out, though bad girl and naughty girl are probably OK). And if she waves you away or rejects your offer of a private or lap dance, then respect her wishes in a polite manner. And remember that no means no.

## Attention

At the other end of the spectrum, make sure that no woman leaves a male strip show feeling neglected or rejected. She may not be the prettiest, wealthiest, youngest or thinnest lady in the room. She may not be the type of gal you picture yourself dating, but — hate to break it to you, dude — this is not your night; it's hers. Make every woman in the crowd feel like a goddess, princess or queen. Regale her with warm and tender smiles, and the hottest of 'sex eyes'. Pin her with an intense gaze that stops just short of a leer, dripping with passion, desire, and seduction. Make her feel like an irresistible beauty, one who has drawn the attention of the most desirable man in the room. Call her your sweetheart and your baby; if she becomes a regular customer, call her by her name and let her know that you appreciate her continued patronage.

### Sweet talk

If you'd like some surefire prompts or primers for talking dirty (but in a tasteful way), here are some suggested phrases that might be helpful:

*You are a beautiful woman.*
*You are so sexy.*
*Your man is one lucky fella; would he mind too much if you had an affair?*
*You make me so hot baby.*
*You turn me on.*
*I want to be your fantasy.*
*Tell me what you want…*
*May I have this dance?*
*I'm so horny, are you?*
*Wanna mess around with me tonight?*
*I've been fantasizing about making you feel good*
*I've always thought it would be fun if you didn't use your hands*
*I'll meet you in the bedroom after I fold the laundry*

### Stay professional

Of course, all of this kissing and cooing, loving and wooing aside, you as a dancer are never under any obligation to tell a customer you love her, to let her touch or view your penis, to divulge your e-mail address or phone number, or to date or sleep with her outside the club. Most reputable male strip groups frown on these behaviors anyway. While you may be a sex object in the eyes of these women, you are still in every way a human being worthy of respect.

If a woman calls you a demeaning name, hurts or slaps you, claws at your back, fondles your private parts, step away from her with a sexy move and make it clear that she crossed the line. Should she not get the message, do not hesitate to report her to the club management and have her removed from the premises.

## Size matters

With all that having been said, the ladies are allowed to admire 'the one big thing' that most women look for in a male exotic dancer. They will want you to have a big shaft or, at the very least, the illusion of one. If you have a sizable cock then show it off, via a G-string, a C-string (you will undoubtfully get their full attention with that) or any other sexy underwear. If you are more modestly endowed, you might consider 'stuffing a sock in it' so to speak, or perhaps even wearing a prosthetic. Or just emphasize whatever you have with some defining underwear or the use of a penis pump.

# TIP #5
# UNDRESS FOR SUCCESS

When it comes to female strippers, it's pretty safe to say that their male fans don't care what they wear on stage, as long as they take it off post haste! For female fans of exotic dance, by contrast, the fantasy is half the fun.

It is not enough for a male exotic dancer to have killer abs, he also must have a killer attitude as well; he must give his audience members a delicious fantasy that will stimulate their minds, their body parts, and of course their wallets!

**Dress to undress**

The costume that you choose will depend entirely on the image you want to convey onstage. You could go with an industry staple and become a cop, a fireman, a doctor, a seaman, or a construction worker. Or you could take things to the next level by transforming yourself into a super hero or a regal prince from another time.

The possibilities are as limitless as your imagination, and of course, as your personal budget.

If you have unlimited funds, you may wish to spend them on some jackets of velvet or satin brocade, fine silk shirts, and pantaloon-style trousers of leather or velvet. Also don't be too macho to experiment with wigs, make up, and costume jewelry. These elaborate costumes could serve to transform you into a nobleman of the Renaissance or Victorian England, a pirate of the high seas, a paranormal lord of the night, or another hero who looks as though he's just stepped off the cover of a romance novel.

At the other end of the spectrum any dude with a basic wardrobe can come up with a costume of some sort. Own a pair of jeans, a tank top, and a muscle T-shirt? You could be a construction worker. Add a basic leather jacket, matching knee high leather boots and gold chains to this mix, and suddenly you are a sexy rock star, there to thrill and tease a room full of your most devoted fans — and all without playing a single note of music! Though if you do happen to have a guitar or microphone on hand, do feel free to favor the ladies with a few bars of a sexy song. They will love it!

Don a simple button down work shirt and some basic work pants, along with a fetching billed hat, and you could appear as a repair man, delivery dude or the seductive boy next door. Or you could fish out the three piece business suit lurking at the back of your closet (the one you pull out for job interviews) to pose as a high powered executive or brash international playboy — or perhaps even a hot male secretary, there to serve his female boss. Just slip on a colorful, tight fitting pair of swimming trunks to become a sensual lifeguard or sexy surfer. Surf's up!

Other more standardized costumes are available online and at costume shops. Whether you want to pose as a police officer, fireman, cowboy, military officer or space alien, you are sure to find the uniforms and the props that will facilitate that goal.

### The wardrobe

Regardless of the specific costume you choose, a good male stripper always must have some basic costume props. These include a strong supply of multi-colored and patterned G-strings and C-strings. Some dancers prefer G's in rainbow colors while others go for basic black or pristine (tee hee hee) ivory. You may also choose animal print G-strings with zebra or leopard patterns for a wild, sensual effect. Roar!

Also required will be multiple pairs of boxer shorts in similar hues; the boxer short is the appealing wrapping that conceals the ultimate gift! Wear them over your G-string as an extra layer to peel off, and an extra step in the level of excitement of your female audience.

Tear away pants — and possibly shirts — are other musts in a stripper's wardrobe. You definitely don't want to rip apart expensive pairs of formal dress pants on a nightly basis. Furthermore you don't want to take the risk of losing your best dress clothes to an over-eager fan who rips them to pieces in passion. These onetime use wardrobe articles bear the appearance of standard pants but they can be ripped off at a moment's notice; thus making it a lot easier to perform a red hot striptease.

Any or all of these items can be ordered online (everywhere from Amazon and Buy.Com to Eastbay.Com) or purchased at an adult book or lingerie store. Certain menswear stores also carry them, along with some general dance supplies stores; after all, even male ballet dancers need G-strings to complete particularly skimpy or revealing costumes.

### Find a theme

In determining the very best costumes to wear for your striptease performances, you should consider several key factors. First and foremost you must think of the ladies. Do they want to see a cop or a fireman? Fabio or Christian Grey? A vampire or an angel? A sheik or a pizza delivery boy? Tarzan or a Calvin Klein model?

To find the answers to these questions, quiz the lady in your life as well as your female relatives and friends. Check the covers of popular romance novels and erotic books aimed at women. Also watch some adult films aimed at females. And we are not talking Busty Bi Biker Babes, vol. 15. We are instead referring to high class productions from the likes of Playgirl, Impulse, Femme, Strawberry Seductress, Chick Media, Good Vibrations' Good Releasing, and New Sensations (the Romance series). These companies produce the explicit visualizations of women's deepest, most secret fantasies; sit up (or lay down!) and take notice!

Also be sure, however, to respect the boundaries of good taste in making your selections. Despite the success of 50 Shades of Grey, think twice before showing up at a male revue show bearing whips, paddles and chains. And while some ladies might entertain fantasies of priests, monks or scholastic headmasters, others might be offended by these costumes and might complain to the club manager and/or take leave of the show and venue. You probably could get away with a sexy devil motif, providing that you stick to a red satin body suit complete with horns and a pitchfork, and avoid any actual religious symbolism.

Ultimately, the costume should represent your fantasy as well as that of your customers. If a tight pair of jeans or an elegant business suit makes you feel sexy and confident, then those qualities are sure to shine through in your performance. And if you always have fantasized about being a particular book or movie character, or a certain fantasy or national hero, then you no doubt will enjoy dressing up as this character; and your audience is sure to enjoy it even more.

Choosing your costume is bound to be one of the most enjoyable components of your new job as a male exotic dancer along, of course, with stripping out of these costumes in the presence of countless adoring ladies!

# TIP #6
## NOW IT'S TIME TO HIT THE STAGE...
## BUT WHERE?

So now you know that you have everything it takes to become the best male stripper in the exotic dance industry. Now exactly where do you plan to showcase your immeasurable talents for the pleasure and benefit of sure to be grateful women?

Well, the answer to this question depends entirely on where you live, or perhaps where you would like to live.

If you live in a major party city like Las Vegas, Los Angeles, New York City or Miami, then becoming a male stripper can be as easy as walking into the friendly neighborhood male strip club, requesting a job application, and an audition time. Soon you may be dancing center stage at an upscale night club, in the theater area of a swanky hotel, or in a free standing structure that operates solely as a male exotic dance club. For more info about how to apply for work with some major troupes, visit Chippendales.com, http://www.aussiestorm.com.au/ (the site for Manpower Australia), LaBare.Com and http://www.hwmen.com/ (the site for Hollywood Men).

Apart from these major cities, however, the sad fact of the matter is that very few communities feature male strip clubs in their business and entertainment districts. Even in Tampa, Florida — widely considered the strip club capital of the world and the setting of "Magic Mike" — one cannot currently find a single club that exists solely for the purpose of presenting male dancers who perform for a female audience. What are prevalent in these communities are male strip groups who perform semi-regularly at night clubs and special events. They also make individual dancers available for private parties like bachelorette fests, feminine birthdays, girls' nights in, etc.

Surf the Internet and let your fingers do the walking in that big yellow book to find male strip groups in your area. You may also consider the possibility of setting up a business as an independent dancer. Sure you'll have to get a business license, set up your own website, and pay for your own photo sessions and costumes. You'll have to do your own advertising, taking out ads in newspapers, adult entertainment websites & periodicals, and women's interest mags & sites in your area. Yet at the end of the day, you set your own hours and keep all your own tips and booking fees.

Regardless of where or to whom you apply for employment, you will need to present pretty much the same information. You will need to supply a recent photo that displays your face and body to good effect. It is strongly suggested that you employ a professional photographer to take these photos.

You also will be asked to supply your full legal name, your age, your address, your 'day job', and to relate any previous dance, modeling or acting experience you may have.

You may be asked as to why you are applying for the job of exotic dancer. Be very careful about your reply. Those who answer "I want money," or "I want lots of sex with hot women", are obviously likely to be rejected sharply and promptly without further consideration. These replies are, to say the least, unprofessional and ungentlemanly. It would be far better to express — and for that matter, to feel — a genuine desire to entertain audiences and to bring pleasure to women. If you like to bring a smile to a woman's face, if you like to show off and make people laugh and have a good time, if you have a theatrical bent, if the women in your life tell you that you'd be good at this sort of thing, then you'll want to highlight these points in your interview.

Once your application is accepted, you may very well be called in for an interview and audition session. Be positive, upbeat, and at all times professional throughout the course of your question and answer session. Treat it with the same respect and dignity that you would any other job interview.

When they ask you to dance, by contrast, feel free to throw all semblances of respect and dignity out the proverbial window. Now is not the time to get shy — show 'em the goods to premium effect, putting your beautiful body, your seductive persona, and your hot moves on full and impressive display.

At the same time, do not overdo your attempts to snare a primo job with the troupe. Do not launch yourself into the lap of the woman auditioning you, simulating blatant sex acts left and right. Keep a respectful distance and treat her to a tease, much like the one that you will be giving her audiences every night from this point forward.

# IN CONCLUSION

As a male exotic dancer, you will stand as the living embodiment of a woman's most secret, decadent fantasy. You will become the perfect lover, the sexy other man, the hot fantasy that keeps her up at night; the man of her dreams, the one she never thought she'd find.

Now she can sneak away for a steamy rendezvous with the man of her fantasy; as a male exotic dancer, you alone hold the key to her ecstasy and, for that matter, to your own incredible success.

At this stage, you have all the tools and info you need to make a distant dream a shining reality — so go for it! Become a male exotic dancer today!

And don't forget to let us know your progress, either as a review on the website where you purchased this guide, or by contacting us using the details in our "Discover" section; we do want to hear from you, and will publish the most exciting success stories of male strippers in a revised edition of this title.

###

# ABOUT THE AUTHOR

Megan Hussey is a feminist erotica writer and editor with nine single-title ebooks, twelve anthology stories, an erotic audio CD, and seven paperback novels in print. From mermen to vampires, Megan's stories feature sexy, kind-natured heroes and strong, real woman heroines.

Megan won an Honorable Mention for Love Romances and More Cafe's 2007 Vampire Book of the Year award, for her book "Under Cover of Night: The First Book of Nuit". She was also a nominee for the Erotic Romance Reviews for Women Golden Shoe Award; and her book The One that Got Away received a Recommended Read rating from the Erotica Readers and Writers Association.

Aside from being an award-winning writer, she is an unabashed fan and proponent of the male strip industry. She lives in Florida.

# FREE EBOOK OFFER

Thank you for purchasing this title.

As a token of appreciation, we are delighted to offer you the eBook version of "How To Become A Male Stripper". The digital version contains a lot of additional references and links for your reading pleasure; just click on the video, music or product references to learn more about them.

To get your free eBook, follow these 3 simple steps:

1. Write a short constructive review of "How To Become A Male Stripper"

2. Send us the link of that verified purchased review to freeebook@mypoutylips.com (that way we can verify that you actually purchased this title)

3. Receive your FREE title!

Author: Megan Hussey

Edited by Angelicka Wallows

Published by My Pouty Lips

© 2013 My Pouty Lips

All Rights Reserved

Learn more about My Pouty Lips on

http://www.mypoutylips.com

Printed in Great Britain
by Amazon.co.uk, Ltd.,
Marston Gate.